**W9-BWX-071**

# Counting by: Twos

Esther Sarfatti

Rourke
Publishing LLC
Vero Beach, Florida 32964

www.rourkepublishing.com

PHOTO CREDITS: © Eileen Hart: title page; © Matej Michelizza: page 3; © Justin Horrocks: page 5; © Imre Cikajlo: page 7; © Michael Tripp: page 9; © Stephen Strathdee: page 11; © Misha Shiyanov: page 13; © Sandra vom Stein: page 17; © Renee Brady: pages 19 and 21; © Chris Johnson: page 23.

Editor: Robert Stengard-Olliges

Cover design by Nicola Stratford.

**Library of Congress Cataloging-in-Publication Data**

Sarfatti, Esther.
  Counting by : twos / Esther Sarfatti.
    p. cm. -- (Concepts)
  ISBN 978-1-60044-524-8 (Hardcover)
  ISBN 978-1-60044-665-8 (Softcover)
  1. Counting--Juvenile literature. I. Title.
  QA113.S3565 2008
  513.2'11--dc22
                        2007014072

Printed in the USA

CG/CG

# Rourke Publishing

www.rourkepublishing.com – rourke@rourkepublishing.com
Post Office Box 3328, Vero Beach, FL 32964

# This is two.

What comes in twos?

5

The bicycle has two wheels.

The owl has two eyes.

The airplane has two wings.

The rabbit has two ears.

The girl has two hands.

15

The bear has two cubs.

16

17

The playground has
two swings.

The girl has two shoes.

20

These two kids are twins.
Counting by twos is fun!

23

# Index

airplane    10
bear    16
bicycle    6
rabbit    12

## Further Reading

Dahl, Michael. *Footprints in the Snow: Counting by Twos.* Picture Window Books, 2005.

Dahl, Michael. *Eggs and Legs: Counting by Twos.* Picture Window Books, 2006.

## Recommended Websites

www.edhelper.com/kindergarten/Number_2.htm

## About the Author

Esther Sarfatti has worked with children's books for over 15 years as an editor and translator. This is her first series as an author. Born in Brooklyn, New York, and brought up in a trilingual home, Esther currently lives with her husband and son in Madrid, Spain.